To: Cheryl my daughter
Best life ever

From: Ma!!
with an open
Heart!!!

Daily Rhyming Inspirations

Let a 2-line rhyme be your daily prime!

Jac Blackman, B.A., M.S.

BALBOA.
PRESS
A DIVISION OF HAY HOUSE

Copyright © 2014 Jac Blackman, B.A., M.S.

All rights reserved. No part of this book may be used or reproduced by any means, graphic, electronic, or mechanical, including photocopying, recording, taping or by any information storage retrieval system without the written permission of the publisher except in the case of brief quotations embodied in critical articles and reviews.

Balboa Press books may be ordered through booksellers or by contacting:

Balboa Press
A Division of Hay House
1663 Liberty Drive
Bloomington, IN 47403
www.balboapress.com
1 (877) 407-4847

Because of the dynamic nature of the Internet, any web addresses or links contained in this book may have changed since publication and may no longer be valid. The views expressed in this work are solely those of the author and do not necessarily reflect the views of the publisher, and the publisher hereby disclaims any responsibility for them.

The author of this book does not dispense medical advice or prescribe the use of any technique as a form of treatment for physical, emotional, or medical problems without the advice of a physician, either directly or indirectly. The intent of the author is only to offer information of a general nature to help you in your quest for emotional and spiritual well-being. In the event you use any of the information in this book for yourself, which is your constitutional right, the author and the publisher assume no responsibility for your actions.

Any people depicted in stock imagery provided by Thinkstock are models, and such images are being used for illustrative purposes only.
Certain stock imagery © Thinkstock.

Printed in the United States of America.

ISBN: 978-1-4525-9498-9 (sc)
ISBN: 978-1-4525-9500-9 (hc)
ISBN: 978-1-4525-9499-6 (e)

Library of Congress Control Number: 2014905598

Balboa Press rev. date: 04/28/2014

Editor: Lara Lavonne Jordan
Photographer: DeAnna Dimmit

These inspirations and affirmations are a loving source of enrichment and enlightenment. Read them and take them in – they will nourish your heart, your mind and your soul.

Reverend Suzy Andrews, Minister at the Foothills Center for Spiritual Living in Arcadia, California

After reading each rhyme, say "Yes Yes Yes", as Kinesiology anchors the thought into your subconscious mind.

January 1
. . . .

"Am I my brother's keeper?" asked another,
And the answer was, "No, you *are* your brother".

January 2
. . . .

A positive attitude is the best way,
And I expect to see good things in my day.

January 3
. . . .

A sense of separation is an illusion, so they say,
And so in spite of our perception, all are one in some way.

January 4
....

Abe Lincoln said, "We'll be as happy as we make up our minds to be,"
And that makes it perfectly clear that my happiness is up to me.

January 5
....

All are my father, mother, sisters and brothers,
For I am clear in my oneness with all others.

January 6
....

All things were made to be different and unique,
So each different person is a Divine speak.

January 7

. . . .

As I focus on the conditions I see,
Somehow more and more of them just seem to be.

January 8

. . . .

As I grow spiritually, more and more I am seeing
The mystical Self present within every other being.

January 9

. . . .

Although I've had negative feelings about the past,
It is up to me whether or not they are to last.

January 10
....

Any sense of separation
Is always our own creation.

January 11
....

As I conquer the body and mind,
Greater realms of peace and joy I find.

January 12
....

As I master the science of deliberate creations,
I greatly accelerate my desired manifestations.

"*Yes! Yes! Yes!*"

January 13

As we perceive,
So we receive.

January 14

Be alert for the good and praise it more and more,
And you get to enjoy more from the Divine store.

January 15

Before I get me out of bed,
I get me right within my head.

January 16
. . . .

Before I put my mouth in gear,
I focus on Love not on Fear.

January 17
. . . .

Before the experience of the Oneness and its love,
We have no idea of the bliss below and above.

January 18
. . . .

Before the world's struggles can possibly cease,
We must learn to live with each other in peace.

January 19
....

Both birth and death are each simply but a door;
On the other side there is more, there is more!

January 20
....

Caring for Mother Earth is our responsibility,
Especially if we would like to continue to be.

January 21
....

Changing focus of our mind and heart
Changes the results that will impart.

January 22
....

Conscious response is now my daily way,
And I am clear in all I do and say.

January 23
....

Contemplation and meditation lead to a deeper inner state,
Where our souls and God can more intimately join and interrelate.

January 24
....

"Created in the image and likeness of God" must mean
I'm a beloved part of the Divine created scene.

January 25

. . . .

Dealing with the core issues of our victim role
Will help us to bring our lives back under control.

January 26

. . . .

Divine protection surrounds me
And helps me to feel safe and free.

January 27

. . . .

"Do unto others as you would have them do unto you";
Clearly there in that saying is one of life's biggest clues.

January 28
. . . .

Each blessed day before I get out of bed,
I check my thoughts that all is right in my head.

January 29
. . . .

Each day I give thanks that I am so blessed
And find that I feel and am much less stressed.

January 30
. . . .

Each meal I bless the food, the day, all life, and Mother Earth,
Grateful that each day brings new blessings, new gifts, and new birth.

January 31
....

Even on cloudy days, I let my positive expectations arise,
For I realize that life may well present an unexpected surprise.

February 1
....

Even though I may feel I'm tossed and torn,
I always find new energy reborn.

February 2
....

Even when another cannot see who you are,
Just remember that you are always a bright star.

February 3
....

Every challenge I may meet in life
Is an invitation to remove strife.

February 4
....

Every day is a new opportunity
Just waiting wide open with good presents for me.

February 5
....

Every day gives my spirits a special lift,
For I can now see each day as a Divine gift.

February 6
....

Every day when I awake I say,
"I decree today a really great day."

February 7
....

Every problem that we may face
Has its own perfect purpose and place.

February 8
....

Every second some part of us dies and is reborn;
Our attitude will either make it a rose or a thorn.

February 9

. . . .

Every time that I see a beautiful view,
I feel like it's God saying to me, "I love you."

February 10

. . . .

Feelings are a precious human part
That helps me to feel God in my heart!

February 11

. . . .

For me to know if there is a God or not,
I must be in my heart—not in my thought.

February 12
. . . .

Forgiving another for some past wrong
Makes us freer, happier, and more strong.

February 13
. . . .

"God helps those who help themselves" is very well known,
And the harvest comes after the seeds have been sown.

February 14
. . . .

Good times frequently seem to come and go,
But universal good is a constant flow.

February 15
....

I accept 100% responsibility
For all of the food and drink that I put inside me.

February 16
....

I accept abundance as my Divine birthright,
And it sets all of my concerns and fears to flight.

February 17
....

I am a clear expression of the Divine
And express my creativity just fine.

February 18

....

I am clear what an intimate relationship should be,
And I use that as a clear model of what to make me.

February 19

....

I am free of old doubts and fears;
My life is full of joys and cheers.

February 20

....

I am free of the negatives of the past,
And I now live my life as a free person at last.

February 21
. . . .

I am generous in love, service, and giving,
And it's a prosperous life that I am living.

February 22
. . . .

I am impeccable with my word,
And I now soar through life like a bird.

February 23
. . . .

I am living the spirit of the Christ every day,
And it changes my every thought and every way.

February 24
....

I am Master to the law and not its slave,
Because of the great example Jesus gave.

February 25
....

I am mastering the "why" and "how",
And I am successful in the "NOW".

February 26
....

I am now clearly seeing the Light;
The good things of life are my birthright.

February 27
....

I am spirit and I am free;
There's no other way I can be!

February 28
....

I anticipate my days as all special days,
And wonderful things come to me in many ways.

March 1
....

I appreciate each moment of every day,
And they come back to me in the most wonderful way.

March 2
. . . .

I clearly see the wonderful vision of God for me,
So I am happy, healthy, and God-aware as can be.

March 3
. . . .

I commit to loving myself unconditionally
And follow the patterns of how the Loving Source loves me.

March 4
. . . .

I create a much greater money attraction
By realizing money is God in action.

March 5
．．．．．．．．．．．．．．．．．．．．．．

I embrace the true image I'm meant to be,
And find that more and more doors open for me.

March 6
．．．．．．．．．．．．．．．．．．．．．．

I expect to make mistakes and to be wrong,
For through my mistakes I'm learning to be strong.

March 7
．．．．．．．．．．．．．．．．．．．．．．

I face the New Year free of fear;
All that I want and need is here.

March 8

. . . .

I feel I'm part of the Divine dance
And experience rich abundance.

March 9

. . . .

I feel so blessed in so many ways,
And I appreciate rich, full days.

March 10

. . . .

I focus on my spiritual life,
And I am now free of fear, stress, and strife.

March 11
....

I have a vision for my personal life and days,
And my life is now reflecting it back in all ways.

March 12
....

I have an appreciative attitude,
And I express it with frequent gratitude.

March 13
....

I have broken the chains that bind;
I am free in body and mind.

March 14

. . . .

I have the power to change every reaction
To experience a more positive attraction.

March 15

. . . .

I hold my friends and family close to my heart,
For every one of them is a priceless part.

March 16

. . . .

I hold myself in a Holy Light,
And my many worries now take flight.

March 17

. . . .

I know I have nothing to fear,
For I know my God is right here.

March 18

. . . .

I know the Divine does not judge its own creations,
For all are part of Its perfect manifestations.

March 19

. . . .

I look back on my life and what do I see—
A someone who needed to learn how to be.

March 20

. . . .

If I want any true chance to be really free,
I must handle my own responsibility.

March 21

. . . .

I now look to the future with joyous expectations,
For I know my life is filled with great manifestations.

March 22

. . . .

I now release my grievance against all others
And view them as my spiritual sisters and brothers.

March 23
. . . .

I permit others to be who and what they are,
For I focus my attention on my own star.

March 24
. . . .

I refuse to use my time to gripe and complain,
For every loss is replaced by a greater gain.

March 25
. . . .

I send daily blessings to Mother Earth,
For from her body came my body's birth.

March 26
....

I see beyond past thought and belief;
My mind is free of old fear and grief.

March 27
....

I see through the eyes of the Divine,
And peace is continually mine.

March 28
....

I speak the word
And know it's heard!

March 29
....

I surrender my burdens to the Divine,
And everything seems to turn out just fine.

March 30
....

I surrender my troubles to the Loving Source,
Knowing that somehow, someway, they're handled, of course.

March 31
....

I surrender my every challenge to Spirit,
Knowing that it is the ultimate Source to clear it.

"Yes! Yes! Yes!"

April 1
....

I take the time to smell the roses,
And Nature her sweetness discloses.

April 2
....

I view every day as a great gift,
And it gives my soul a daily uplift.

April 3
....

I was not made to fit someone else's mold,
So I stand tall in my being—clear and bold.

April 4
....

I watch the foods I put on my plate
And am my ideal figure and weight.

April 5
....

If I have a feeling of being apart,
I get in touch with myself in my own heart.

April 6
....

If I want unconditional love to come to me,
Then that is the formula of just what I must be.

April 7
. . . .

If the changes for the better are to be,
It's going to be all up to you and me.

April 8
. . . .

If the Divine is really all-present as they have said,
Then we need to clear all negative judgments from our head.

April 9
. . . .

I'm filled with love and free of fear;
My life is a "go" and in high gear!

April 10
....

I'm responsible for every feeling and thought,
And they exactly predetermine what I have bought.

April 11
....

In all persons, things, moon, and sun,
I know that there is only the One.

April 12
....

In all things I do my best,
And to God I leave the rest.

April 13
....

In balancing life between human and the Divine,
I constantly use discipline in this life of mine.

April 14
....

In God I trust;
Success is a must!

April 15
....

In spite of all the things I may have done,
I am still bathed in the love of the One.

April 16
....

In the Oneness of my spiritual family,
God becomes even easier for me to see.

April 17
....

In the pure smile of the baby's face
Lies the hope of the whole human race.

April 18
....

In this life it is primarily my attitude
That determines my life's longitude and latitude.

April 19
....

It appears the this life is a school,
And we need to live the Golden Rule.

April 20
....

It is better to have loved and lost;
Who has not loved has paid a great cost.

April 21
....

It is only as we commit to face our fear
That we find our spiritual courage is already here.

April 22

....

It is only our hearts and minds
That in the last resolve frees or binds.

April 23

....

It is only the poor, ignorant fool
Who thinks self-criticism's a good tool.

April 24

....

It is our choice which path we take in life,
The God-inspired one or the one of strife.

April 25
....

It is the clearer vision of the Divine that now fills my life and mind,
And I experience prosperity of a much greater kind.

April 26
....

Judgment of another makes us angry,
And we find that we are the one not free.

April 27
....

Life can be pleasant or gory,
But it is all our own story.

April 28

. . . .

Life is so good and life is so great—
Totally there to appreciate.

April 29

. . . .

Life or death may present a different face,
But everything is still in the One's place.

April 30

. . . .

Life's direction may sometimes seem to hide,
But I can rely on my inner guide.

"Yes! Yes! Yes!"

May 1
....

Many of the areas we need to heal in life
Are experienced through our interpersonal strife.

May 2
....

Meditation, prayers, and right thoughts and deeds
Drive my spiritual growth like faithful steeds.

May 3
....

Mercy brings greatness to all hearts
And respects all like equal parts.

May 4

....

Music stirs our hearts and souls, and emotions rise
To lift each one in love on a Divine surprise.

May 5

....

My attitude determines my type of day,
So I look at all life as a Divine play.

May 6

....

My body is strong, vibrant, and healthy,
And I feel happy, loving, and wealthy.

May 7

. . . .

My body is vibrant, healthy, and strong;
I function on full-charge all the day long.

May 8

. . . .

My communications with all others and you
Is what I am contributing to the world view.

May 9

. . . .

My gratitude fills my being,
Knowing what I'll soon be seeing.

"*Yes!   Yes!   Yes!*"

May 10
....

My heart overflows with joy and thanks;
I now live life running on full tanks.

May 11
....

My intimate relationship radiates unconditional love;
The God within has raised this earthly bond to dimensions high above.

May 12
....

My life is under spiritual direction,
And gives to me a wonderful life-projection.

May 13

....

My mind and heart are wide open to serve and give,
For that is the way I am committed to live.

May 14

....

My mind focuses on the Oneness of all things,
And my happiness, peace, and joy now find new wings.

May 15

....

My mind is free of fear, anger, and depressions,
For my focus is on the positive expressions.

"Yes! Yes! Yes!"

May 16

. . . .

My perceptions are true and clear;
Clarity is mine now and here.

May 17

. . . .

My prayer's most important part
Is right here deep in my heart.

May 18

. . . .

My prosperity increases on steady courses
From many expected and unexpected sources.

"*Yes!   Yes!   Yes!*"

May 19

....

My thoughts are like a command to the Universe,
Which correspondingly empties or fills my purse.

May 20

....

My thoughts are like the steering reins leading a pack of horses,
For it is my thoughts and not the horses that set my courses.

May 21

....

No essentials of life and accomplishment are omitted
When the mind and heart have made themselves totally committed.

May 22

....

No matter what may come my way this day,
My faith and courage help me be okay.

May 23

....

No matter what may face me,
I'm as peaceful as can be.

May 24

....

Now I have my divinely ideal mate;
The relationship is divinely great!

"*Yes!*   *Yes!*   *Yes!*"

May 25
. . . .

One is all and all are one,
Like the rays of our own sun.

May 26
. . . .

Open hearts help change a life
When they're in the midst of strife.

May 27
. . . .

My greatest disasters or challenges or strife
Often bring me the greatest blessings in my life.

May 28
....

Out of the depth of despair within my soul,
The power of Spirit reaches within to make me whole.

May 29
....

Out of the stark darkness comes the Light,
And my spirit takes delighted flight.

May 30
....

I pay attention and after a while it's plain to see,
I will be as happy as I make up my mind to be.

"*Yes!* *Yes!* *Yes!*"

May 31

....

Personally and spiritually, I am growing
With a superb radiance that is brilliantly showing.

June 1

....

Prayer uses the very power of the Universe
And a very good thing to have, for sure, in the purse.

June 2

....

Roses are red, violets are blue,
And all's rosy pink when I'm with you.

June 3
. . . .

Science says that all things vibrate,
And so the Divine did create.

June 4
. . . .

Science says there are at least eleven Universes;
I wonder where all those people go who leave in hearses.

June 5
. . . .

Service is a path to help us find
The greater gifts of both heart and mind.

June 6
. . . .

Shakespeare mentioned about the many lives and stages;
Our beliefs determine the content of the pages.

June 7
. . . .

Since my beliefs are the prelude to my path,
I think I'll give them all a good cleansing bath.

June 8
. . . .

Since prosperity is that which I seek,
I cannot afford a doubt or fear leak.

"Yes! Yes! Yes!"

June 9
....

Socrates said, "The wise person knows that he knows nothing,"
And when he knows he knows that, he finally knows something.

June 10
....

Some people often put themselves down;
No wonder they live life with a frown.

June 11
....

Sometimes in our life's challenges or storms,
We find our own angels in many forms.

June 12
....

Sometimes deep inside I know
Just where my life needs to go.

June 13
....

Spirit provides me clear guidance in my life,
And so I am happier and free of strife.

June 14
....

The 50,000 thoughts we think every day
Are the details that end up paving life's way.

June 15
. . . .

The answers that I seek to find
Are already known in my mind.

June 16
. . . .

The answers to life that we seek
Can be found by an inner peek.

June 17
. . . .

The Buddha wisdom guides my day;
It makes clear my daily way.

"Yes! Yes! Yes!"

June 18
....

The Buddhist lesson of detachment
Facilitates my Divine attachment.

June 19
....

The child within is so precious to see;
It keeps me as healthy as I can be.

June 20
....

The Collective Consciousness does not limit me;
Through truth and wisdom I'm as free as I can be.

June 21
....

The deep essence of the mystic calls from within me,
And I strive to be the best spirit that I can be.

June 22
....

The direction I let thoughts or prayers roam
Determines where they will find a new home.

June 23
....

The errors of the past are over and dead,
And I refuse to permit them in my head.

June 24
....

The example of Jesus and His ways
Is the guide for me in each of my days.

June 25
....

The fire of Spirit runs through my soul,
And I feel joy and totally whole.

June 26
....

The garbage I project on others on my path
Is suggesting my own unresolved pain and wrath.

June 27
....

The gifts that we share in our very generous giving
Are returned to us many times over in our living.

June 28
....

The good life's our birthright to enjoy:
Health, love, peace, prosperity, and joy.

June 29
....

The happiness I seek in every day
Lies in all that I think, feel, believe, and say.

June 30
. . . .

The head must be the servant of the heart,
Or all of our plans will get blown apart.

July 1
. . . .

The holy Jihad or internal struggle within me
Is producing the evolving spirit I choose to be.

July 2
. . . .

The image that I hold within my mind
Is the reality that I will find.

July 3
. . . .

The Infinite Spirit and the human are one,
As surely as the sun's rays are part of the sun.

July 4
. . . .

The key to our forward movement
Is now in this Holy moment.

July 5
. . . .

The kindness and generosities I share for other's needs
Sprout forth reciprocal harvest from such loving and sweet seeds.

"Yes! Yes! Yes!"

July 6
....

The Master's hand has touched my soul,
And I am peaceful, happy, and whole.

July 7
....

The mental equivalent I hold in mind
Is the desired end result that I now find.

July 8
....

The miracles of life are all ours to share,
As we realize they are already there.

July 9

....

The more we smile and the happier we are,
The higher we can raise our body's health bar.

July 10

....

The negative programs that controlled me in the past
Have been released with a gigantic spiritual blast.

July 11

....

The only Father that has ever been or ever will be
Is the role model which our hearts have endlessly yearned to see.

July 12

. . . .

The path of spirit is many ways,
And we see gifts for all in all days.

July 13

. . . .

The place to find love is within,
For then our love is a sure win.

July 14

. . . .

The purpose of my life is now totally clear,
And I live life boldly and richly without fear.

July 15
....

The questions of life do not leave me high and dry,
For Spirit within me knows the how, when, and why.

July 16
....

The realization of just who and what we are
Raises us out of our dust and up to our own star!

July 17
....

The reason people say it is better to have loved and lost
Is because those who have not loved have paid a very great cost.

July 18
. . . .

The reason people say, "Oh, don't cry,"
Is because of the feelings they deny.

July 19
. . . .

The regard with which I hold you
Reflects back my own inner view.

July 20
. . . .

The rigidities and judgments of my mind
Are places I leave my love and peace behind.

July 21
. . . .

The server gets served and the giver is given;
That's the simple rule of the life we are livin.'

July 22
. . . .

The positive things that I do and say
Are paving the way for a better day.

July 23
. . . .

The total day's emotion and thought
Are shown in all that the day has wrought.

July 24
. . . .

The teachings of the Master's way
Are the guide for every day.

July 25
. . . .

The teachings of Jesus, an exceptional man,
Provide the ideal guide for my day-to-day plan.

July 26
. . . .

The universal principles are my daily tools to use.
With such exquisite gifts to use, how can I possibly lose?

July 27
....

The very answers I seek to find
Are already known within my mind.

July 28
....

The very judgment I put on another being
Is a reflection of my own essence I'm seeing.

July 29
....

The very things I seek to create, attract, and find
Already lie waiting in the depths of my own mind.

July 30
. . . .

The very words that we share with others
Can help to heal our sisters and brothers.

July 31
. . . .

The view I hold of life and myself in my secret thought
Is the reality that I discover I have bought.

August 1
. . . .

The vision of the Divine is clear in my mind,
And I leave all concerns and worries far behind.

August 2
....

The way that I perceive life
Brings me joy or brings me strife.

August 3
....

The way to have loving friends around me
Is for me to be that which I want to see.

August 4
....

The words we speak and the things we say
Affect our world in so many ways.

August 5
. . . .

The words we use each day
All have their own display.

August 6
. . . .

There is a practitioner deep within my heart;
It knows that God and I can never be apart.

August 7
. . . .

There is a Universal Law,
And it always works without flaw.

August 8

. . . .

There is one life within which all exist,
And realizing this lifts us to bliss.

August 9

. . . .

There is only one family on planet Earth,
And every single person has equal worth.

August 10

. . . .

There may be many religions under God's sun,
But the way we live our life is the only one.

August 11

....

There is only one Power and Source,
And its answer to our prayers is, "Of course!"

August 12

....

There's no lack in the Divine store;
There's always more. There's always more.

August 13

....

This great Universe has its own unique design
And even includes your unique design and mine.

August 14

. . . .

Through understanding how the law really works,
I now significantly increase my perks.

August 15

. . . .

Through my deep introspection, there is revealed to me
More of the greater magnificence that I can be.

August 16

. . . .

Through the greater truths I believe,
I find it easy to receive.

"Yes!   Yes!   Yes!"

August 17
. . . .

To expand my consciousness level or range,
I positively accept the pending change.

August 18
. . . .

Today I know the purpose and blessings of my soul,
And my life is happy, healthy, prosperous, and whole.

August 19
. . . .

Unconditional love flows to and from me;
I'm as loving and loved as I can now be.

August 20
....

"United we stand and divided we will fall"
Guides us to stand as all for one and one for all.

August 21
....

We are already one with the Supreme;
Anything less is simply our own dream.

August 22
....

We know that no one is an island,
For all are one in the Divine plan.

August 23

....

We prime a pump to make it flow,
And that is just how our lives go.

August 24

....

We understand the true vision of the global heart,
As each one of us awakens and becomes our part.

August 25

....

We're one with our Creator;
What could be greater?

August 26

....

What I feel about me I will project on you;
My rejection or love always shows in full view.

August 27

....

What I may have considered a challenge before
Is now opportunity knocking on my door.

August 28

....

That which I within myself see
Is what I think others to be.

August 29
....

Whatever I may lovingly give away
Is reciprocated back to me some day.

August 30
....

Whatever I practice for my self-talk
Is always the prelude of my self-walk.

August 31
....

Whatever it is that I may in any way put out
Returns in one way or another in my input spout.

September 1

. . . .

What does it take to feel the Presence of the Creator?
Simply eliminate our own inner separator.

September 2

. . . .

When I am in touch with my feelings,
It is the prelude to my healings.

September 3

. . . .

When I can have belief in myself,
I'm like a precious book on the shelf.

September 4
. . . .

When I feel the Universal Presence in another,
It's clear that everyone is my sister or brother.

September 5
. . . .

When I judge another for something I may see,
It's a projection from the unresolved in me.

September 6
. . . .

When I judge another, I just judge me;
That is the obvious for all to see.

September 7
. . . .

When I let go and let God,
It's like a seed in the sod.

September 8
. . . .

When I share with another from a loving space,
I add something special to the whole human race.

September 9
. . . .

When life presents us with grief,
Supporting friends bring relief.

September 10
. . . .

When my work makes me feel just like a jerk,
It's time to jerk myself out of that work.

September 11
. . . .

When the blues try to pop into my head,
I focus on my gratitude instead.

September 12
. . . .

When the minds of our precious youth are questioning and reaching,
We are present with caring and love and meaningful teaching.

September 13
....

When we let our hearts be open,
We find we are then better copin'.

September 14
....

Whenever a difficulty may arise,
I just expect a quick solution surprise.

September 15
....

Whenever I feel my creativity is blocked,
I let the flow of Spirit get it quickly unlocked.

September 16

. . . .

Whenever I have a goal to do,
I keep the end result clear in view.

September 17

. . . .

Whenever I have an irritated feeling,
I know it's an invitation to self-healing.

September 18

. . . .

Whenever I have some creation I want to see,
I declare creativity flows freely through me.

September 19
. . . .

Whenever I have troubles or sorrow to face,
I always go to the calm of that inner place.

September 20
. . . .

Whenever I may feel my creativity is locked up,
I remind myself that the Divine is never blocked up.

September 21
. . . .

Whenever I seek an inspirational part,
I only need to look deep within my own heart.

September 22
. . . .

Whenever things get a bit tight,
I'd rather be loving than right.

September 23
. . . .

Whenever we gripe and complain,
We invite more of the same pain.

September 24
. . . .

Whenever we hang out with bring-me-downs,
Instead of smiles, we will end up with frowns.

September 25
....

Whenever you are growing and experiencing pain,
Just remember every loss must have a greater gain.

September 26
....

Where my focus or thought goes
Is where my energy flows.

September 27
....

Whether you will live your life by power or by force
Depends on whether you align with the Loving Source.

September 28

....

Whether the day is up or the day is down,
I greet either with a smile and not a frown.

September 29

....

Who knows all the ways of the loving God;
Our prayers are like seeds in that Divine sod.

September 30

....

With a sense of the Divine in my heart,
I know that I am an integral part.

October 1
....

With God as my Source,
The answer's "Of course!"

October 2
....

With great reverence I hold my beloved in my heart,
And the Divine love then permeates through every part.

October 3
....

With healthy self-esteem,
I can now really beam.

"Yes! Yes! Yes!"

October 4
....

With much greater attention on my day's acts,
I change lesser to greater in my life's facts.

October 5
....

With negativity seemingly all around,
I look for the positive I know can be found.

October 6
....

With the practice of inclusive love for one and all,
Negatives, greed, violence, and fear all fall.

October 7

....

Without a vision, a nation will perish;
Our vision is one we nurture and cherish.

October 8

....

You and I and the moon and the sun—
The many are really just the One.

October 9

....

You may judge the way people are and what they do,
But another's private life is not up to you.

October 10
....

Every thought, belief, feeling, and emotion
Triggers the Universal Law into motion.

October 11
....

The Law of the Universe responds correspondingly to our thought,
And as we look at our life, we see just exactly what we have wrought.

October 12
....

When any artist takes up a brush,
It's because there is a Divine rush.

October 13
. . . .

We hold our opinions as though they were truth,
Even though most are other's thoughts from our youth.

October 14
. . . .

I keep my spirits happy and high,
And I can feel my very soul fly.

October 15
. . . .

The greatest hope for any generation
Is to remove the sense of separation.

October 16
. . . .

When there's no judgment left in me,
I am as free as I can be.

October 17
. . . .

Everything visible comes from the invisible,
Because all creation comes from the indivisible.

October 18
. . . .

"It is done as you believe" is what we hear,
And the result of our beliefs is now here.

October 19

When we begin to feel the Divine Presence,
We begin to understand our own essence.

October 20

When we have loved, we have never loved in vain,
For any love helps to ease another's pain.

October 21

Because I have lived pain like you feel,
My compassion starts to help you heal.

October 22

....

If I have hurt you in the past,
I pray your pains no longer last.

October 23

....

Why did they ever compare you, do you suppose,
When we cannot compare a lily and a rose?

October 24

....

I felt the Oneness of the Divine,
And it reassured me all was fine.

October 25
....

Unconditional love is the greatest gift to give,
For it helps free another person to really live.

October 26
....

I can't judge another without judging myself,
So I think I'll just put all judgment on the shelf.

October 27
....

I'll no longer be what someone else thinks that I should be;
I'll live my life as the great Creator created me.

October 28
....

Inspirational leaders tell us to be in the 'now';
When I am in the creative flow, I understand how.

October 29
....

I bless my food, the day, the Earth, and every living thing,
For I understand the blessed blessings that my blessings bring.

October 30
....

As I behold the marvels of the Earth,
A new sense of being seems to take birth.

October 31

....

As I grow, I know every loss must have a greater gain,
And greater peace and joy are replacing my previous pain.

November 1

....

The inner child is such a great gift,
For it gives all our lives such a lift.

November 2

....

I see each day as a greater opportunity
For the much greater me that I can be.

November 3

. . . .

"Everyone is doing the best they can" is a saying,
So, instead of judging, maybe we just need to be praying.

November 4

. . . .

The exuberant child is still fully alive in me,
And I give it frequent opportunities to be free.

November 5

. . . .

When our life is full of sadness, anger, and strife,
It's high time to change our thinking and change our life.

November 6

....

If you're looking for someone to love you,
Look in the mirror and get a clear view.

November 7

....

Lucky, lucky, lucky me; I'm such a lucky son of a gun.
I think I'll make that line my daily motto and have lots of fun.

November 8

....

Love, power, and wisdom are the mighty three
That we need to live life fully to be free.

November 9
. . . .

In our early life, our opinions are oh, so very sure,
And only later do we realize we were immature.

November 10
. . . .

Divine creativity is a constant flow,
And every day I just see it go and go.

November 11
. . . .

The more we say that we don't know
Is just the way that it will go.

November 12

The more I can love myself in a humble, reverent way,
The greater view of the Universal I'll see in my day.

November 13

The feelings that we deny
Are the ones that make us cry.

November 14

A little love or a little smile
Can help us to go another mile.

November 15
. . . .

When it seems there's no time in the day,
I just let Spirit show me the way.

November 16
. . . .

Letting go of my judgments from the past
Shows me I'm the one who is free at last.

November 17
. . . .

Our greatest challenges and disasters
Often lead us to become self-masters.

November 18
....

Wherever our thoughts may go
Is where the energies flow.

November 19
....

The sum of our beliefs
Precedes our joys and griefs.

November 20
....

Everyday is a new opportunity
For me to be all that I can possibly be.

"*Yes!* *Yes!* *Yes!*"

November 21
....

I readily face any fear
For I know that my God is here.

November 22
....

When I have a tough challenge to face
I let Spirit fill that very place.

November 23
....

If fear tries to raise its head,
I let Spirit strike it dead.

November 24
. . . .

Handle all with greatest care,
For God is everywhere.

November 25
. . . .

Every thought and feeling is a prayer to some degree,
So I'll manage my thoughts and feelings to set myself free.

November 26
. . . .

I give my angers from present and past
A totally eradicating blast.

November 27
. . . .

Fear, judgment, and negativity
Can only bring a much lesser me.

November 28
. . . .

I will bravely face any fear I must,
And leave it all behind me in the dust.

November 29
. . . .

Every day has a better start
When I greet it with an open heart.

November 30

....

With a ready smile on my face,
I can help lift the human race.

December 1

....

Our differences are all Divine, not damned,
For that's the way the Universe was planned.

December 2

....

Hearts filled with love and mirth
Make for a better Earth.

December 3
....

Whenever we meet someone who needs a lift,
Unconditional love is a priceless gift.

December 4
....

A heart full of joy
Is a Divine toy.

December 5
....

Amazed, I saw a stone wall vibrate one day,
And then I thought, science says "It's all that way."

December 6
....

For a person who may be suffering depression,
A walk in the sunshine brings a sunny impression.

December 7
....

The beauty of the mountain trees, sun, and lake
Can transform us and make our very soul quake.

December 8
....

The love of our family and friends
Helps take us through life's challenging bends.

December 9

....

I am divinely guided in all I think, say and do,
And no matter what challenges I face, my path is true.

December 10

....

I feel safe knowing I am divinely protected in all ways,
And I experience great joy and ease as I go through my days.

December 11

....

I keep positive thoughts in my mind,
And it's a far better life I find.

December 12
. . . .

I'm very conscious about what I put on my plate
And easily maintain my ideal figure and weight.

December 13
. . . .

I put all self-criticism on the lam
And accept myself just the way that I am.

December 14
. . . .

I'm in the ideal place doing my ideal thing,
And I'm so happy I can now feel my heart sing.

December 15
....

My spiritual body in all of its perfection
Is manifesting through me in every direction.

December 16
....

I love my sweetheart unconditionally,
And that same level of love comes back to me.

December 17
....

I feel like the Divine storehouse has over-spilled,
And I'm happy, healthy, prosperous, and fulfilled.

December 18
. . . .

In my family, work, priorities, time, and health,
I have an ideal balance that is like priceless wealth.

December 19
. . . .

I listen closely to what others say,
And I notice they treat me the same way.

December 20
. . . .

Endless blessings seem to pour over me,
And I am as grateful as I can be.

December 21
....

My prosperity is steadily increasing,
And any concerns are steadily releasing.

December 22
....

I am generous in my giving
And see the returns in my living.

December 23
....

My body is healthy, vibrant, and strong,
And my mind is sharp and clear all day long.

December 24
....

I have sharp, clear, wonderful recall,
Remembering names, faces, and all.

December 25
....

My self-discipline is quite ideal,
And very great peace is what I feel.

December 26
....

I know my intuition is always right,
And I follow its guide for every flight.

December 27
....

I gladly donate at least 10% of my income,
For I recognize the abundant Source it comes from.

December 28
....

My communications are a two-way street
With a clarity that just can not be beat.

December 29
....

I am now able to express my complete self,
For all other roles were put away on the shelf.

December 30
. . . .

I ensure my wants and needs are fully expressed
In communication that's lovingly addressed.

December 31
. . . .

No matter what the situation may be,
I handle conflict management superbly.

CPSIA information can be obtained at www.ICGtesting.com
Printed in the USA
LVOW06s1146200514

386563LV00001B/1/P